GENOCIDE IN MODERN TIMES™

GENOCIDE IN DARFUR

Janey Levy

ROSEN
PUBLISHING®

New York

To the people of Darfur

Published in 2009 by The Rosen Publishing Group, Inc.
29 East 21st Street, New York, NY 10010

Library of Congress Cataloging-in-Publication Data

Levy, Janey.
Genocide in Darfur / Janey Levy.
    p. cm. — (Genocide in modern times)
Includes bibliographical references and index.
ISBN-13: 978-1-4042-1824-6 (library binding)
1. Genocide—Sudan—Darfur. 2. Sudan—History—Darfur Conflict,
2003– 3. Darfur (Sudan)—Ethnic relations. I. Title.
DT159.6.D27L48 2008
962.404'3—dc22

                                                    2007048352

Manufactured in the United States of America

On the cover: Background: Displaced Sudanese wait to receive food supplies from the World Food Program in Nyala, Sudan. Foreground: An armed Sudanese rebel arrives at Chero Kasi after Janjaweed militiamen set it ablaze.

CONTENTS

INTRODUCTION

You may have heard the term "genocide" in a history class or in the news. However, you may not be sure exactly what it means. Officially, genocide is defined as the systematic attempt to destroy a group of people because of their nationality, ethnic origin, race, or religion. However, some people apply it more broadly to any intentional government-sponsored murder of a distinct group of people for any reason.

The term comes from combining the Greek word *genos*, which means "race," "tribe," or "nation," with the Latin *cide*, which means "killing." So "genocide" literally means killing a race, tribe, or nation. Dr. Raphael Lemkin, a Polish lawyer, coined the term. He first used it in a 1944 book about Nazi policies in Germany and its conquered territories during World War II.

Although the term first appeared in 1944, the practice of genocide has existed for thousands of years. An early example

These women are returning to the Mourni camp in West Darfur carrying loads of firewood on their heads. They risk rape or death each time they leave the camp. Mourni is one of the largest camps for internally displaced persons (IDPs). More than 70,000 IDPs live there.

from recorded history occurred in 416 BCE. The great Greek city of Athens attacked the island of Melos and committed genocide against its citizens.

The Albigensian Crusade of 1209 is sometimes called the first genocide of modern times. You may not think of something that happened eight hundred years ago as "modern." However, here the word just means "not ancient," something that happened in the last few hundred years rather than something that happened thousands of years ago.

A crusade was a holy war called by the pope, the leader of the Catholic Church, against enemies of the faith. An enemy of the faith was anyone who disagreed with the Catholic Church's teachings. In the Albigensian Crusade, Catholic soldiers attacked and killed Christians who held different beliefs.

Numerous genocides occurred during the twentieth century. The first took place in 1915, when Turkey destroyed the country's Armenian population. Perhaps the most infamous genocide of the twentieth century was the Holocaust of World War II, when Nazi Germany killed six million Jews, along with millions of others. At the end of the twentieth century, genocide in Rwanda left 800,000 Rwandans dead.

The early twenty-first century genocide in Sudan's Darfur region is yet another entry in this tragic catalog. The violence began in February 2002, when African groups in Darfur launched a rebellion against Sudan's Arab-controlled government. Government soldiers fought the rebellion with the aid of government-armed militias drawn from nomadic Arab tribes. The militias were known as Janjaweed— "devils on horseback." Religion wasn't the issue, since all the groups involved were Muslims. Rather, the Arab-dominated government and Janjaweed declared their goal was to rid Darfur of Africans. Government soldiers and Janjaweed militias forced more than two million Africans from their homes. As many as 500,000 Africans may have died. The Darfur genocide has been called the worst humanitarian crisis of the early twenty-first century.

1

A Brief History of Genocide

Dr. Raphael Lemkin, the man who invented the term "genocide," was born in Poland in 1900 or 1901. After completing a law degree in 1926, Lemkin became a government attorney in Poland. When Germany invaded Poland in 1939, he joined the resistance fighters. He later fled to Sweden, then to the United States, where he arrived in 1941. Lemkin spent much of his professional life writing about genocide and trying to convince the world's nations to make it a crime under international law.

Propelled by the horrors of the 1915 Armenian genocide and the Iraqi government's 1933 massacre of Iraqi Christians, Lemkin launched an international campaign to outlaw such atrocities. At a 1933 conference on international law held in Madrid, Spain, Lemkin urged that these "acts of barbarity" be condemned as crimes against humanity. He was unsuccessful, but he refused to abandon his campaign. By 1944, when he published his most famous book, *Axis Rule in Occupied Europe*, he had created a special term for these barbarous acts—genocide. Genocide was recognized as a war crime at the Nuremberg Trials (1945–1949) following World War II.

Lemkin was not satisfied with having genocide recognized only as a war crime, however. He also wanted it acknowledged as a crime when committed in peacetime. In 1948, he finally succeeded in

Raphael Lemkin campaigned tirelessly to get the world to recognize genocide as a crime. He is shown here in 1950, two years after the United Nations finally approved the Convention on the Prevention and Punishment of the Crime of Genocide.

convincing the United Nations to make genocide a crime under international law. This meant that the international community could punish those who committed genocide no matter when they carried it out.

GENOCIDE FROM ANCIENT TIMES THROUGH WORLD WAR II

Genocide has probably been practiced since before there was written history. One of the earliest recorded genocides occurred in 416 BCE during the Second Peloponnesian War. The war, fought between the ancient Greek cities of Athens and Sparta, takes its name from the region where it occurred—the southern Greek peninsula known as the Peloponnesus. The island of Melos, once a Spartan colony, tried to remain neutral during the war. However, Athens demanded that Melos submit to Athenian rule and pay tribute money. When the people of Melos refused, the Athenians attacked the island, killed all the men, made slaves of the women and children, and gave the island to Athenian settlers.

The 1209 Albigensian Crusade pitted Christian against Christian. Southern France was home to a group of people whose version of Christianity was contrary to official Catholic teachings and thus considered heresy. After failing to destroy the heresy through peaceful means, the

At the Battle of Muret, Catholic forces led by Simon de Montfort defeated "heretics" led by Raymond of Toulouse. This illustration of the battle comes from a manuscript on the history of France created around 1375.

pope called a crusade against the heretics. Thousands of soldiers from northern Europe descended on southern France. They destroyed cities and crops, and exterminated thousands of people. In one town, for example, crusaders killed 15,000 men, women, and children.

In 1913, a coup in Turkey swept a trio of dictators into power. They wanted to build an empire by expanding east, a path that would take them through the homeland of about two million Armenians. Islamic extremists in Turkey decided the best way to achieve their dream of an empire was to eliminate the Christian Armenians blocking their way. By 1918, up to 1.5 million Armenians had been killed and the rest driven away. Turks quickly took over the homes and villages once occupied by Armenians.

In 1933, Christian Assyrians in Muslim Iraq suffered a similar fate. Many of the Assyrians had been forced into refugee camps during conflicts from 1914 to 1923. In 1933, the Iraqi government told them they must either relocate to tiny villages scattered among the hostile Muslim population or leave the country. When several hundred Assyrians tried to leave, Iraqi border troops attacked and killed them. The troops then executed unarmed Assyrians in surrounding villages while the Iraqi government did nothing. In the end, more than 3,000 Assyrians were killed.

Convention on the Prevention and Punishment of the Crime of Genocide

In December 1948, the United Nations approved a convention, or agreement, on genocide. The convention went into effect in January 1951. It made genocide a crime under international law and defined it this way (as quoted by the Web site for the UN Office of the High Commissioner for Human Rights):

In the present Convention, genocide means any of the following acts committed with intent to destroy, in whole or in part, a national, ethnical, racial, or religious group, as such:

(a) Killing members of the group;
(b) Causing serious bodily or mental harm to members of the group;
(c) Deliberately inflicting on the group conditions of life calculated to bring about its physical destruction in whole or in part;
(d) Imposing measures intended to prevent births within the group;
(e) Forcibly transferring children of the group to another group.

For many people, the word "genocide" first brings to mind the Holocaust of World War II. Under Adolf Hitler, Germany's Nazi rulers systematically murdered millions of people they considered inferior in some way. The Nazis focused especially on Jews. Their goal was to kill every Jewish man, woman, and child under German rule. It was the religious aspect of the persecution, combined with the fact that many victims' bodies were burned, that led to the use of the term "Holocaust." The word is a religious term that means "a burnt sacrificial offering." In addition to Jews, Nazis targeted other groups, including Polish people and Roma, or Gypsies. By the time the war ended, the Nazis had murdered perhaps eleven million people, including about six million Jews.

GENOCIDE AFTER WORLD WAR II

The 1945–1949 Nuremberg Trials established genocide as a war crime. The 1948 Convention on the Prevention and Punishment of the Crime of Genocide made it an international crime regardless of whether it occurred during wartime or peacetime. Seemingly, the world had been put on notice that the community of nations would no longer tolerate genocide. In spite of this, the second half of the twentieth century saw numerous instances of genocide.

Nazi leaders Hermann Göring, Rudolf Hess, Joachim von Ribbentrop, Wilhelm Keitel, and Alfred Rosenberg are seated in the front row of the defendants box at the Nuremberg Trials. All but Hess were found guilty of genocide.

The International Criminal Court

The International Criminal Court (ICC) was created to try individuals accused of genocide, war crimes, and crimes against humanity. Its focus on individuals distinguishes it from the International Court of Justice, which handles disputes between countries. The ICC was established in 1998 at a conference of nations held in Rome, Italy. It came into being in 2002, after sixty countries had approved the agreement establishing the court. Its headquarters are in The Hague, the Netherlands. In 2007, the court announced charges stemming from the Darfur atrocities.

From 1975 to 1979, Pol Pot and the Communist Khmer Rouge ruled the Southeast Asian nation of Cambodia. Their radical goal was to create a pure, classless peasant society. The government expelled all foreigners and forced Cambodians living in cities to move to the countryside. They banned all religions and persecuted ethnic and religious minorities such as the Vietnamese, Chinese, Muslims, and Buddhist monks. No one knows for sure how many people were executed or died from disease, starvation, and overwork. Estimates range from one million to over three million.

Between 1981 and 1983, the Guatemalan government carried out what is sometimes called the Silent Holocaust against the nation's Mayan Indians. Over the course of a civil war that lasted from 1962 to 1996, more than 200,000 people were killed or disappeared. About 83 percent were Maya. The attacks on the Maya were particularly intense between 1981 and 1983. The government claimed the Maya were aiding rebel forces. However, many victims were children, making it clear the government's real purpose was to destroy the Maya. Soldiers tortured and killed Maya and destroyed villages and crops.

In an effort to heal the wounds left from the brutal Guatemalan civil war, bodies of genocide victims were dug up so they could be identified and properly buried. These Maya are carrying the coffins of sixty-six victims for reburial. Their remains were dug up from at least six different mass grave sites.

The Republic of Bosnia and Herzegovina, once part of the southeast European nation of Yugoslavia, became independent in 1992. Almost immediately, the government began a campaign of genocide against the nation's Muslims and Croats (people from the neighboring country of Croatia). Thousands of Muslim and Croat civilians were imprisoned, expelled, attacked, tortured, and murdered. Their homes, businesses, and places of worship were destroyed. The genocide finally ended in 1995.

During the same period of the Bosnia and Herzegovina genocide, a swift and savage genocide occurred in the central African nation of Rwanda. Problems had long existed between the country's two major ethnic groups, the Tutsis and the Hutus. In 1994, the president, a Hutu, died when his plane was shot down. Within hours, violence erupted. By the time the violence ended about 100 days later, around 800,000 people had been killed. Most of the dead were Tutsis. Most of the killers were Hutus.

2

Sudan's Path to Genocide

The Republic of Sudan, located in northeast Africa, is the continent's largest country, covering about 976,500 square miles (2,529,123 square kilometers). It's composed of nine states, including Darfur. The northern and southern parts of the country differ significantly. Most of Sudan's people and cities are in the northern two-thirds of the country. Most northern people consider themselves "Arab," whether they are descendants of earlier Arab immigrants or Africans who adopted Arab language and culture. The remaining northern people are considered "African." All northern people are Muslim. In contrast, the south is mostly rural and has many fewer people. The people are considered "African." Most practice traditional African religions or are Christian.

Darfur is in western Sudan. The name "Darfur" means "home of the Fur." *Dar* is the Arabic word for "home." The Fur are the region's dominant ethnic group. The other principal ethnic groups are the Zaghawa and Masalit. Arabs arrived in Darfur between the fourteenth and eighteenth centuries. So much intermarriage between Arabs and native ethnic groups occurred over the centuries that there is now little physical difference between "Arabs" and "Africans." In northern Sudan, both "Arabs" and "Africans" are Muslim.

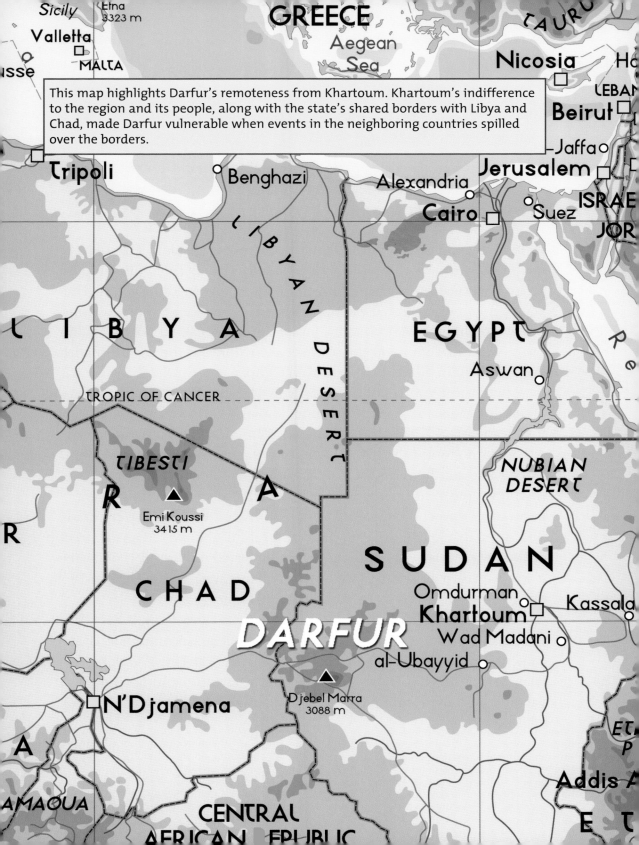

This map highlights Darfur's remoteness from Khartoum. Khartoum's indifference to the region and its people, along with the state's shared borders with Libya and Chad, made Darfur vulnerable when events in the neighboring countries spilled over the borders.

Sicily

Etna
3323 m

GREECE

TAURU

Valletta

MALTA

Aegean
Sea

Nicosia

Ho

LEBAN

usse

Beirut

Tripoli

Benghazi

Alexandria

Jaffa

Jerusalem

ISRAE

Cairo

Suez

JOR

L I B Y A N

LIBYAN DESERT

EGYPT

Aswan

Re

TROPIC OF CANCER

TIBESTI

R R A

NUBIAN
DESERT

Emi Koussi
3415 m

A

SUDAN

CHAD

Omdurman

Kassala

Khartoum

DARFUR

Wad Madani

al-Ubayyid

N'Djamena

Djebel Marra
3088 m

ET

A

Addis A

AMAOUA

CENTRAL
AFRICAN REPUBLIC

E

Sudan has been independent since 1956. However, the journey that led to Sudan's genocide in Darfur began in the late 1800s. It's a complicated tale that involves conquest; internal politics; social, ethnic, racial, and regional tensions; religious extremism; drought, famine, and desertification; civil wars; and the political ambitions of other countries.

SUDAN'S POLITICAL HISTORY

In 1898, Britain and Egypt took joint control over Sudan. This didn't include Darfur, which was an independent territory ruled by a sultan. Egypt governed northern Sudan, and Britain governed the south. The arrangement exaggerated existing differences between the two regions. Egypt encouraged Islamic values in the Arabic-speaking north. Britain promoted Christianity in the south and encouraged the use of English. In 1916, Britain added Darfur to the territory it controlled.

After World War II ended in 1945, Britain and Egypt began preparing Sudan for independence. They united Sudan's various regions. The northern city of Khartoum became the capital, and wealthy northern Arabs from around the Nile River received control of the government. Darfur and southern Sudan were excluded from any real power.

Sudan received independence in 1956. However, establishing a permanent government seemed impossible, and the country endured prolonged instability. In 1958, General Ibrahim Abboud led an army coup of the government. Abboud's government lasted only until 1964, when it was overthrown and replaced by a civilian government. Then in 1969, the army again seized control and made Colonel Jaafar Nimeiri the country's leader. Nimeiri's government lasted sixteen years. After a brief period of civilian government, General Omar Hassan Ahmad al-Bashir came to power in a 1989 coup organized by the extremist National Islamic Front (NIF). Darfur, remote from Khartoum and having no valuable resources, suffered neglect from all these governments.

President Omar Hassan al-Bashir appears at a rally in 1992. He had just returned from a development conference in Darfur and promised peace in the nation. At the same time, his government was arming and training ethnic militias to fight the rebels in the south.

THE PURSUIT OF AN ISLAMIC STATE

Ever since Sudan's independence, extremists have zealously pursued a policy of Arabization and Islamization. The result for Sudan's people has been suffering on a massive scale. However, it's important to remember the extremists' beliefs don't represent those of all Sudan's Arabs and Muslims. Tens of thousands of the radicals' victims have been Muslims. Many of Sudan's Arabs have actively opposed the extremists' policies.

Efforts to Islamize southern Sudan began under General Ibrahim Abboud in 1958. In 1964, the radical Muslim Brotherhood formed. Its goal was to create an Islamic state. Islamists gained government positions in the 1970s, and their influence spread. In 1983, Khartoum approved the "September laws," which imposed strict Islamic law on all Sudan. The early 1980s also saw the formation of a supremacist group called the Arab Gathering, or Arab Alliance. In addition, the NIF—the Muslim Brotherhood's political party—became a powerful force in the government. The NIF wanted to make Sudan a key center of the radical Islamic world. Under its influence, Sudan hosted meetings of terrorists and became the home of Osama bin Laden from 1991 to 1996. Most Arab governments shunned the extremist Sudan.

NATURAL DISASTERS

Climate has played a major role in Darfur's settlement patterns and cultural development. The south, which receives 32 to 55 inches (810 to 1,400 millimeters) of rain annually, is home to farmers and cattle-herding nomads. Camel-herding nomads wander the far north, which receives only about 4 inches (100 mm) of rain annually. Other parts of the north, which may receive up to 32 inches (810 mm) of rain, have farms and industry. Northern nomads moved south to graze their camels in farmland during the dry season. They bought grain from farmers and carried the farmers' goods to distant markets. A series of natural disasters altered these traditional rhythms of life.

The natural disasters that plagued Sudan throughout the twentieth century had particularly devastating effects in Darfur. Drought, water shortages, crop destruction by locusts, famine, and disease were recurring problems. In *Darfur's Sorrow: A History of Destruction and Genocide*, M. W. Daly reports that up to 25 percent of the Fur died in a 1926 disease outbreak. Daly also estimates that more than 100,000 Darfurians died

This man crouches over land ravaged in the early 1990s by one of Sudan's recurring droughts. The drought resulted in a major famine. Food promised to the people of Darfur never arrived, leading to widespread starvation.

during drought and famine in 1984 and 1985. In addition, desertification spread in the far north.

The continuing drought and desertification affected northern nomads the most. People and animals were forced to permanently move south in search of water and grazing land. This migration placed environmental stress on lands already occupied by farmers. It also led to competition for increasingly limited resources and fueled tension between ethnic groups.

NORTH AGAINST SOUTH

In 1958, Abboud's campaign of Islamization and Arabization led to civil war. Southern rebels formed a guerrilla army called Anya Nya, which means "snake poison." The war finally ended in 1972, when Khartoum and Anya Nya signed a peace treaty.

In 1983, Khartoum broke the treaty, and civil war erupted again. The discovery of oil in southern Sudan gave Khartoum even more reason to

SPLM/SPLA leader John Garang appears in this 1986 photograph. After the Comprehensive Peace Agreement (CPA) was signed in 2005, he became Sudan's vice president. He died in a helicopter crash just weeks after taking office.

seek control of the region. The Sudan People's Liberation Movement (SPLM) and the Sudan People's Liberation Army (SPLA), led by John Garang, headed the south's rebellion.

In response, Khartoum developed tactics it would continue to use in its quest to Islamize and Arabize the entire country. The government armed and trained ethnic militias to fight the rebels and civilians who supported them. It also used rebel armies from other countries. In addition, Khartoum—in violation of international law—used starvation as a weapon of war by preventing aid workers from delivering food to people in the south. According to Don Cheadle and John Prendergast in *Not on Our Watch*, more than 500,000 people starved to death in 1992 and 1993.

Under pressure from the United States and other countries, peace talks began in 2001. The two sides finally signed the Comprehensive Peace Agreement (CPA) in 2005. It called for the north and south to share power for six years, at which time the south would vote on self-determination. It also stated Islamic law would not be imposed on the south. Unfortunately, the CPA began to fall apart in late 2007. The

SPLM complained that Khartoum was not fulfilling the agreement and withdrew from the joint government.

LIBYA, CHAD, AND DARFUR'S TROUBLES

Libya's territorial ambitions and political events in Chad had a profound effect on neighboring Darfur. Libya's Colonel Muammar Qaddafi dreamed of an extremist Islamic empire across Africa. He planned to first take over Chad. Taking advantage of Chad's long-running civil war, Qaddafi sent guns through Darfur to the Chadian rebels. Khartoum supported the rebels as well and allowed them to hide in Darfur. Chadian refugees also settled in Darfur. The rebels and refugees strained Darfur's resources. Drought and desertification in the north had already driven Zaghawa and Arab nomads into central and southern Darfur, putting heavy demands on the resources there.

Chad's government troops pursued the rebels into Darfur. Libya saw another opportunity to further its pursuit of empire. It provided weapons to Darfur's Zaghawa and Arab nomads. It also fueled Darfur's ethnic tensions with propaganda about how "Africans" had denied "Arabs"

Muammar Qaddafi appears here on a visit to Dakar, Senegal, in 1985. Qaddafi came to power in Libya in 1969 after leading a coup that overthrew the monarchy. Although Qaddafi holds no official title in Libya's government, he functions as the head of state.

their rights. Concerned the propaganda might lead to violence, the Fur organized militias for self-protection. Chad's government supplied arms to them. In 1987, war erupted between Fur militias and the Arab Janjaweed. It ended in 1989, but Janjaweed attacks on "African" villages continued.

Darfur's situation worsened after the NIF came to power in 1989. Libya agreed to provide military aid to the NIF in its civil war with southern Sudan. In exchange, the NIF allowed Libya to use Darfur as a base from which to build its empire. Fighting across Darfur's border with Chad intensified. Chadians destroyed Fur and Zaghawa villages.

The Lost Boys of Sudan

The second civil war between Khartoum and southern Sudan produced a generation of orphans and boys separated from their families. Known as the Lost Boys, they were forced to flee to avoid slavery, death, or being forced to fight for Khartoum. They walked hundreds of miles to reach refugee camps in Ethiopia. Ten thousand reached the camps, but thousands of others had died on the journey. Then the Ethiopian government was overthrown in 1991, and the boys had to flee again. Sixteen thousand boys—and some girls—reached Kakuma refugee camp in Kenya. Others went to other Kenyan camps. In 2000, the U.S. government began to bring some of the Lost Boys to America.

DARFURIANS DECIDE TO ACT

In May 2000, the so-called *Black Book* was published. The unknown authors presented facts demonstrating that Khartoum's neglect of Darfur and other regions remote from the capital was intentional. The book's goal was to move the Sudanese people to take action that would bring about profound change in Sudan. It had a significant effect in Darfur. The book helped unite Darfurians from different backgrounds and ethnic groups who wanted to force changes that would aid Darfur. In 2001, a group of leaders formed the Justice and Equality Movement (JEM). JEM called for radical constitutional reform and increased power for neglected regions.

Also in 2001, Fur and Zaghawa rebel leaders formed the Darfur Liberation Front (DLF) to fight the NIF and Janjaweed. The Masalit joined the DLF later that year. In February 2002, the DLF launched its first battle. It attacked and destroyed a government post. Organized rebellion had begun. Khartoum responded with a massive genocide campaign.

3

Genocide in Darfur

After the February 2002 DLF attack on the government post, Fur leaders presented a list of Janjaweed atrocities to the Khartoum government. Khartoum made some insincere efforts to negotiate peace with the rebels. It was really just buying time to organize its plans. Meanwhile, Janjaweed attacks continued.

In October 2002, the DLF elected leaders. They included representatives of the Fur, Zaghawa, and Masalit tribes, as well as several Arabs. The DLF slowly transformed into the Sudan Liberation Movement (SLM) and the Sudan Liberation Army (SLA). In February 2003, the SLA attacked a government garrison and killed 200 soldiers. The following month, the SLM/SLA issued a manifesto spelling out its goals. It called for a secular state and self-determination for Darfur. It condemned oppression and urged Darfur's Arabs to join the SLM/SLA in bringing about a "New Sudan."

For the next several months, the SLA and JEM enjoyed a series of victories against the government and Janjaweed. However, the situation soon began to change. At first, the government and Janjaweed had focused most of their attacks on rebel camps. In mid-2003, they began to concentrate their attacks on civilians. The genocide had begun.

THE GOVERNMENT'S PLAN

The SLA and JEM experienced so many victories against government soldiers in early 2003 because they fought a guerrilla-style war. The regular Sudanese army could not successfully combat this type of fighting. The government recognized that it needed to employ a different approach to defeat the rebels. Khartoum declared a state of emergency and arrested hundreds of rebel supporters. It also created a plan to use the Janjaweed to fight the rebels. The army would provide assistance, but the Janjaweed would do the major fighting. This would allow the government to claim the fighting in Darfur was just the usual tribal conflict and the government was not responsible for it. At the same time, it would allow Khartoum to accomplish its goal: driving all "Africans" out of Darfur. The government knew what the results of using the Janjaweed would be. They had used similar militias during the civil war with the south and had seen what happened there.

The government recruited for the Janjaweed among the Arab tribes and paid Arab sheikhs for their support, offering cash and promising future development to improve the tribes' lives. However, in spite of the government's efforts, some Arab tribes refused to take part in the genocide.

Any non-Arabs who tried to join the Janjaweed were rejected. However, any Arabs at all—including criminals—were accepted. In fact, the government actively recruited criminals for the Janjaweed. Khartoum also took steps to improve the Janjaweed's fighting abilities. It provided weapons, communications equipment, military advisers, and training.

GENOCIDE

Attacks on civilians by the Janjaweed and government soldiers increased even as fighting with the rebels declined. Soldiers and the Janjaweed commonly worked together. Soldiers bombed a village or town, then the Janjaweed moved in. After the Janjaweed were finished, soldiers killed

This 2004 photograph shows a Janjaweed fighter riding in Darfur near the border with Chad. The well-armed fighter brandishes an automatic weapon supplied by the Sudanese government. Terrified civilians fleeing on foot had no hope of escaping fighters on horseback.

or captured anyone left alive. There's evidence soldiers used chemical weapons in their attacks.

The Janjaweed tortured, shot, and stabbed civilians. They shouted racial slurs and called their victims "slaves." They shouted claims that the land belonged to "Arabs," not to "Africans." The Janjaweed sometimes lined up men and boys and shot them in the back of the head. They tossed children into burning houses. They chained schoolchildren together and burned them alive. Women and girls were raped, often more than once. Some rape victims were killed, some were not. For the women and girls of Darfur, rape was not only a horrific experience but also a source of great shame. In order to make their suffering worse, the

Janjaweed sometimes branded rape victims so that everyone who saw them would know what had happened to them.

Villagers who managed to escape or survive Janjaweed attacks lost everything. The Janjaweed took anything of value in the villages and towns. They destroyed clinics, schools, mosques, and entire villages. They even tore apart copies of the Koran, the Muslims' holy book. They stole or destroyed food and animals. They poisoned the water by throwing dead bodies into wells. They wanted to leave nothing for survivors to return to. After they had finished, Arabs sometimes settled on the land and gave the place a new name in Arabic.

This is all that remains of the Darfurian village of Chero Kasi after the Janjaweed burned it down in 2004. Such total destruction was in keeping with their policy of permanently driving survivors out by leaving nothing for them to return to.

The Janjaweed burned down the village of Tundubai in 2004. People in the area fled to neighboring Chad seeking safety. Tundubai was abandoned by its residents and is slowly being reclaimed by the desert.

Why did local officials do nothing to stop the genocide? Khartoum had issued orders not to interfere with the Janjaweed. In fact, Khartoum ordered local officials to give the Janjaweed whatever they needed. In addition, many police and government officials simply left Darfur. Civilians had no protection except what the SLA and JEM could offer.

When word of what was happening in Darfur finally reached the outside world, Khartoum at first simply denied it. The government claimed the stories were lies and propaganda that reflected the Western world's bias against Arabs and Islam. Finally, Khartoum agreed to cooperate with aid agencies trying to get food and other supplies to refugees and internally displaced persons (IDPs). Then the government delayed the delivery of food and supplies. Khartoum also tried to deceive the world into believing it was taking action to halt the genocide in Darfur. It arranged fake handovers of Janjaweed weapons for reporters to witness. It took convicts from prison, proclaimed they were Janjaweed, and executed them. All the while, the genocide continued.

Since Khartoum kept reporters and aid workers out of Darfur, it was hard to know how many refugees and IDPs there were. Since the Janjaweed threw bodies down wells, burned them, or buried them in mass graves, it was hard to know how many had been killed. It's estimated that up to 500,000 were killed. Chad sheltered 200,000 or more refugees. Inside Darfur, there were approximately two million IDPs.

PEACE EFFORTS

Efforts were made to end the atrocities. In 2003, the president of Chad got both sides to agree to a forty-five-day cease-fire so that aid could be delivered to refugees and IDPs. Unfortunately, neither side honored the cease-fire.

Attacks on Aid Workers

Even aid workers, whose only goal was to help refugees and IDPs, were not safe in Darfur. Fighting sometimes forced them to leave areas where their help was needed. Their bases were attacked. Their vehicles were attacked or stolen to prevent them from reaching people who needed aid. In 2006, more than 100 vehicles belonging to aid workers were stolen. Aid supplies were also stolen. Even workers themselves were attacked. At least thirteen aid workers were killed in 2006.

New peace talks were held in 2004. This time the African Union (AU)—a group of African nations that promotes cooperation and provides aid to member nations—also took part. Another cease-fire was reached. It called for the government to disarm the Janjaweed and provide aid agencies with full access to refugees and IDPs. It also established a

African Union leader Alfa Omar Conary visits President al-Bashir *(left)* in Khartoum in August 2004. Conary helped persuade al-Bashir to participate in the doomed 2004 peace talks with the Darfur rebels.

committee to monitor the cease-fire. In addition, it called for AU peacekeepers in Darfur. However, the peacekeepers were authorized to protect only the cease-fire monitoring committee. They had no authority to protect the people of Darfur. Just as happened with the 2003 cease-fire, neither side honored this temporary peace agreement.

Attempts to reach a permanent peace deal continued in 2005. The efforts were complicated by the fact that the rebels found it increasingly difficult to act in a unified fashion, with a single voice. Different groups had different ideas, and the SLA broke into separate units. In January 2006, the AU called for the United Nations to take over its role in Darfur. Khartoum didn't want this. The government feared it would lose control and never regain it. So Khartoum finally signed the Darfur Peace Agreement (DPA). Unlike the earlier agreements, the DPA was not simply a cease-fire. It established a framework for peace and security, required Khartoum to disarm the Janjaweed, and called for constitutional changes affecting the entire country. Unfortunately, only one unit of the divided SLA signed the agreement. In the end, the DPA proved no more effective at halting the violence than the earlier agreements. Fighting and the suffering of Darfur's people continued.

4

Victims and Aggressors

Khartoum worked hard to keep the genocide in Darfur a secret. The government kept out aid workers and reporters. It punished anyone who published information about the events or spoke with outsiders. However, Khartoum could not prevent aid workers and reporters from reaching the refugees who flooded into Chad. Slowly, stories about the horrors in Darfur reached the outside world.

VICTIMS' STORIES

In *Darfur: A Short History of a Long War*, Julie Flint and Alex de Waal recount a story of a 2004 Janjaweed attack told by a young man who survived. The young man told how the Janjaweed executed a group of the village's young men. The Janjaweed cut the throat of the young man's mother. They raped and killed his oldest sister. They killed his brother and father. They threw all the bodies in the well. The young man was the only member of his family to survive. He escaped execution by hiding under a dead mule.

Flint and de Waal also report another man's story about two attacks his village suffered in 2003. The Janjaweed came alone the

A nomad's camels and goats move toward a watering hole during the early 1990s' drought in Sudan. The recurring droughts created water shortages and destroyed farmland and grazing land. Instead of providing aid, Sudan's government took advantage of the heightened tensions between nomads and farmers to further the goals of Arabization and Islamization.

Angel of Death. At the top was Musa Hilal, the "captain of all captains" and an Arab Gathering leader. He taught new recruits that civilians from the rebels' tribes were also enemies, and he supervised many attacks on civilians himself.

THE GOVERNMENT'S ROLE

Musa Hilal received orders directly from Khartoum. The government denied it, but Hilal didn't. The Janjaweed operated with the government's

37

A Janjaweed fighter visits with police officers at a weekly animal market. The Janjaweed fighter is recognizable by his uniform. It is identical to that of the Sudanese army but lacks the military emblems a soldier would have. The animal market where the men are talking is in Mistiria, Musa Hilal's hometown and command base.

authorization and support. The government head during the genocide in Darfur was General Omar Hassan Ahmad al-Bashir, who came to power in a 1989 military coup.

After fighting erupted in Darfur in 2002, al-Bashir publicly vowed to use the army, police, and Janjaweed to destroy the rebellion. In this and his other decisions, he was following the extremist National Islamic Front (NIF), the leading power in the government.

The NIF was committed to making Sudan an Islamic state by any means possible. They were even willing to conduct jihad against other

Muslims. When the people of Darfur sought government protection against Arab militia attacks in the 1990s, the NIF ignored them. The NIF put Musa Hilal in charge of the Janjaweed and armed and trained them. The NIF instructed local officials in Darfur not to interfere with the Janjaweed but to give them whatever they needed.

The NIF's leader was Hassan al-Turabi. Off and on, al-Turabi held official positions in the government. However, regardless of his official position, al-Turabi was responsible for developing plans and policies for the NIF's Islamic state.

Ali Osman Mohammed Taha's job was to direct implementation of al-Turabi's plans and policies. He held several powerful government

Hassan al-Turabi is shown lecturing in Khartoum in this photograph from December 2000. Although he was no longer speaker of the parliament, he still exercised considerable power in Sudan.

positions and finally became al-Bashir's vice president. Hilal considered Ali Osman the Hero of Sudan.

Under the NIF, the government imposed forced starvation on Darfur's displaced people. Such use of starvation as a weapon of war violates international law, but the NIF didn't care. The government found many ways to delay aid and aid workers. Workers had to receive visas to enter the country. Then they had to get travel and fuel permits. Health workers had to fulfill exacting registration requirements. Medicines had to be tested for "safety." Delivery of workers' vehicles was delayed. When the vehicles finally reached Darfur, the government often seized them. When food at last reached the camps, armed men "guarding" the camps took the food for themselves. These "guards" sometimes didn't even allow IDPs to bring in wild food they had gathered. Khartoum clearly meant to achieve its stated goal of removing all "Africans" from Darfur in order to make it "Arab" and "Islamic."

5

World Response to Darfur's Tragedy

In 2003, the Arab Gathering's political committee issued a confidential report emphasizing the importance of keeping events in Darfur secret. Khartoum recognized the need for secrecy as well. It also counted on the world being preoccupied with events in the south and preferring to ignore Darfur. For a while, it seemed Khartoum might be right. Other nations were eager for peace talks between Khartoum and southern rebels to succeed because they wanted the south's oil. They appeared not to know or care about Darfur. However, as word about the genocide spread, nations, groups, and individuals began pressuring Khartoum to end it. The United States has been a leader in this effort.

GOVERNMENT SUPPRESSION OF NEWS

Khartoum took extreme steps to suppress information about the genocide in Darfur. It prohibited Sudanese journalists from reporting the atrocities. Newspapers that published information about Darfur were censored and punished. Even reporters who wrote stories about rebel attacks were threatened or arrested.

Khartoum denied visas to foreign reporters or didn't allow them to travel to Darfur. Sudanese who talked to foreign reporters or

The Sudanese government arrested even foreign journalists in its efforts to keep events in Darfur secret. Paul Salopek was arrested while on assignment for *National Geographic* magazine in 2006. The government charged Salopek with spying, passing information illegally, writing "false news," and entering the country without a visa. Salopek was released about a month after his arrest.

aid workers were arrested and jailed. Aid workers who were suspected of leaking information might be forced to leave the country. Khartoum shut down Al Jazeera, the world's most watched Arabic-language television station, after it broke the news about the atrocities in Darfur.

In spite of Khartoum's efforts, some aid workers and journalists reached Darfur, and stories about the genocide began to leak out. Reporters and aid workers also learned what was happening from refugees in Chad. Khartoum had no power to block access to the refugees, so it tried to keep more Darfurians from reaching Chad. The government offered money to the Masalit living along the border to prevent Darfurians from entering Chad. The Masalit refused. In response, the government burned Masalit villages and sent soldiers to patrol the border. Still, refugees reached Chad, and reporters and aid workers crossed the border from Chad into Darfur. Khartoum stepped up its efforts. More Sudanese were arrested on suspicion of passing information to foreigners. The government even posted police outside a hospital to keep reporters from talking to patients injured in Janjaweed attacks. In the end, however, Khartoum couldn't keep the genocide secret.

FOREIGN PRESS REPORTS

Foreign journalists' early reports weren't very accurate. Many accounts were written from distant places such as Nairobi, Kenya, or Johannesburg, South Africa, where reporters could get only third-hand information. Eventually, more experienced reporters went directly to Khartoum, Chad,

New York Times op-ed writer Nicholas Kristof was the first U.S. reporter to write extensively about the genocide in Darfur. He's shown here at a 2007 event organized by former president Bill Clinton to discuss a range of social issues. Also shown is Angelina Jolie, one of many celebrities who took up Darfur's cause.

and Darfur. However, it was still a full two years after the first Darfur Liberation Front attack in 2002 before foreign newspapers published detailed articles about the genocide.

New York Times op-ed writer Nicholas Kristof began reporting on Darfur in March 2004. He initially agreed to do a single story on refugees in Chad after hearing about them from aid workers. Shocked by what he learned when he visited the camps, Kristof began a personal campaign to bring the genocide to public attention and force the U.S. government to take action. Many people have credited Kristof with bringing the story into the open. He won a Pulitzer Prize in 2006 for his columns on Darfur.

About the same time Kristof began writing about Darfur, newspapers in Europe also began to devote more attention to the genocide. *Le Monde* presented detailed accounts to the people of France. In Britain, the *Guardian* led the way in reporting events.

U.S. television networks were slow to cover the genocide and gave little airtime to the story. According to Prevent Genocide International, in June 2005, the major U.S. networks aired fifty times as many stories

Life for Refugees and IDPs

Arabs sheltered some IDPs who reached Arab regions. However, most refugees and IDPs lived in camps. Sometimes, the camps were created for them by aid agencies. Sometimes, they created the camps themselves. If they were lucky, they got food and supplies from aid agencies. Unfortunately, many Darfurian refugees and IDPs were not lucky. Safety was also a problem in the camps. Women and girls who left the camps to search for food, water, or firewood could be raped or killed by the Janjaweed. The Janjaweed even attacked the camps. At the end of 2004, conditions in the camps were so bad that one United Nations (UN) official estimated 10,000 people were dying in them every month.

about Michael Jackson as they did about Darfur. They aired twelve times as many stories about Tom Cruise.

RAISING AWARENESS, PRESSING FOR ACTION

As news about Darfur emerged in 2004, numerous groups and individuals began efforts to raise public awareness and press for government action. A meeting of forty nonprofit organizations in July 2004 led to the formation of the Save Darfur Coalition. The coalition grew to include over 180 organizations representing 130 million people. It engaged in public education, mobilized citizens to pressure government leaders, ran television ads, and suggested actions people could take.

College students also formed organizations. In 2004, Nate Wright, Martha Heinemann, and Ben Bixby created Students Taking Action Now: Darfur (STAND). STAND worked to increase awareness and raise funds and campaigned for a political solution to the conflict. Mark Hanis and Andrew Sniderman organized the Genocide Intervention Fund (GIF) to raise money to support the African Union peacekeeping force. Early in 2005, Wright, Stephanie Nyombayire from GIF, and film student Andrew Karlsruher traveled to the border between Chad and Darfur to make a film about the refugees' plight. Funding was provided by mtvU, part of MTV. Later in 2005, STAND and GIF united to form the Genocide Intervention Network (GI-Net), which conducted fund-raising and public education. It also mobilized high school and college students through its more than 800 chapters of STAND.

Individuals as well as groups sought to raise awareness and promote action. Eric Reeves, a professor of English, began writing about Sudan during the civil war between Khartoum and the south. He later turned his attention to the Darfur genocide. He wrote numerous articles, presented evidence to Congress, and gave lectures around the country. Brian Steidle, who served with the 2004 cease-fire monitoring committee, wrote a book, made a film, and gave numerous lectures. Actor Don Cheadle and former

Eric Reeves is shown in his Massachusetts home, surrounded by photographs of Sudanese people. Although Reeves is a full-time college professor of English, he has devoted much of his time to writing and lecturing about Sudan in an effort to raise awareness and inspire people to act.

government official John Prendergast traveled in Darfur, wrote a book, and gave lectures.

Cheadle wasn't the only celebrity who took up Darfur's cause. Angelina Jolie is a Goodwill Ambassador for the United Nations High Commissioner for Refugees (UNHCR) as well as a movie star. She visited refugee camps in Chad, met with government officials, and took part in conferences around the world.

Actor George Clooney traveled to Sudan and Chad, appeared on *Oprah*, held a press conference with senators Barack Obama and Sam Brownback, and addressed the UN Security Council. Actor Mia Farrow visited Darfur and Chad and wrote numerous op-ed articles. Actor Mira Sorvino addressed Congress about the plight of women in Darfur and helped organize a concert to raise money and awareness. Numerous other celebrities also acted on Darfur's behalf. Some people criticized the celebrities, saying none of their actions actually helped Darfur's people. Others believed celebrity involvement drew more attention to the cause and thus helped raise awareness.

In 2004, Mia Farrow visited the Kalma camp for IDPs in southern Darfur. Her visit was intended to draw media and public attention to the terrible situation in Darfur and the dreadful suffering of its people. Here, she's shown singing with a group of children from the camp.

THE CONTINUED SEARCH FOR PEACE

The AU peacekeeping mission begun in 2004 floundered. It had authority to protect only the monitoring committee, not civilians. It had too few troops and too little money. In 2006, the AU publicly called for the UN to take over peacekeeping in Darfur. Khartoum resisted the idea, refusing to allow UN forces in Sudan. Finally, however, after enormous international pressure, Khartoum agreed to admit a UN peacekeeping force. In summer 2007, the UN authorized a force of 26,000, to work under the direction

Members of "the Elders" delegation are shown at a press conference following a meeting with Sudanese president Omar al-Bashir. From left to right, they are former UN diplomat Lakhdar Brahimi, former U.S. president Jimmy Carter, and former South African archbishop Desmond Tutu. Not shown is Graca Machel, the wife of former South African president Nelson Mandela.

of the AU alongside the existing AU force. About half the UN forces arrived January 1, 2008. However, they lacked helicopters and other heavy equipment necessary for the mission. Khartoum's actions also threatened the mission. After agreeing to accept the UN forces, Khartoum then decided it would not admit soldiers from certain countries. Khartoum also tried to delay the UN forces present from reaching Darfur.

In early October 2007, a group of world leaders known as "the Elders" visited Sudan to promote peace and urge all parties to attend the new round of peace talks scheduled for the end of October. The group included former U.S. president Jimmy Carter and Desmond Tutu, a South African leader and winner of the 1984 Nobel Peace Prize. Though their mission was to encourage a political solution to the conflict, they were outspoken in their criticism of the government after visiting Darfur. They also urged Western countries to provide strong support for the joint AU-UN peacekeeping force.

Unfortunately, obstacles continued to block peace efforts. In late September 2007, a group of rebels attacked an AU base, killing ten peacekeepers and wounding several more. In response, government soldiers launched revenge attacks on two Darfur towns.

What You Can Do to Stop Genocide

Here are some things you can do to help stop genocide in Darfur and wherever else it occurs:

- Write to the president urging that the United States act to end the genocide.
- Write to Congress.
- Get involved with organizations working to end genocide.
- Attend an event.
- Organize an event.
- Help raise awareness by telling family and friends about the genocide.
- Help raise money.

When peace talks began in Tripoli, Libya, in late October 2007, only twenty rebels were present. The main rebel leaders refused to attend. One of those leaders announced he would not attend talks until the joint AU-UN peacekeeping force was in place. In late January 2008, after half the UN soldiers were in Sudan to provide security, trucks carrying food aid to Darfur were attacked, and both food and trucks were stolen.

As the search for peace continued, more than two million refugees and IDPs waited for a chance to return to what was left of their homes. They waited in crowded camps under dreadful conditions, with little food, water, and medical care. They waited for the world to care enough to stop the genocide.

TIMELINE

Fourteenth to eighteenth centuries Arab nomads arrive in Darfur. Cattle-herding nomads settle in the south, where they receive land. Camel-herding nomads settle in the north. They don't receive land.

1898 Egypt and Britain take joint control of Sudan (not including Darfur). Egypt administers northern Sudan; Britain administers the south.

Twentieth century Drought, desertification, water shortages, crop destruction by locusts, famine, and disease are recurring problems throughout the century. Darfur suffers intensely. Northern Arab nomads suffer the most. Poverty greatly increases among nomads. Over time, nomads move into central and southern Darfur, straining resources.

1916 Britain takes control of Darfur.

1945 Egypt and Britain begin preparing Sudan for independence. They make the northern city of Khartoum the capital and give control of the government to wealthy northern Arabs from around the Nile River.

1956 Sudan becomes independent.

1958 General Ibrahim Abboud seizes control in a coup. He begins a campaign to Islamize southern Sudan.

1962 Civil war begins in Chad. Chadian rebels and refugees come to Darfur, straining resources. Chadian soldiers follow rebels into Darfur. Chad stirs tensions between "Arabs" and "Africans" in Darfur with propaganda.

1964 Abboud's government is overthrown and replaced by a civilian government. The radical Muslim Brotherhood forms. Its goal is to create an Islamic state.

1969 Colonel Jaafar Nimeiri takes control in a coup. Under him, Islamists are appointed to government positions. Their influence spreads.

1980s Supremacist group called the Arab Gathering, or Arab Alliance, forms. The National Islamic Front (NIF) becomes a powerful force in the government.

1983 Khartoum approves "September laws," which impose strict Islamic law on all Sudan.

1985 Nimeiri's government is overthrown and replaced with a civilian government.

1987–1989 War in Darfur between Fur militias and the Arab Janjaweed. Janjaweed attacks continue after war ends.

1989 The NIF organizes a coup that brings General Omar Hassan Ahmad al-Bashir to power. The NIF allows Libya to use Darfur as a base for building its empire. Chad destroys Darfurian villages.

2000 *Black Book* is published. It recounts government neglect of Darfur.

2001 Justice and Equality Movement (JEM) forms in Darfur. Fur, Zaghawa, and Masalit rebel leaders form the Darfur Liberation Front (DLF).

2002 The DLF attacks a government post, starting a civil war between Darfur and government and Janjaweed forces.

2003 The DLF becomes the Sudan Liberation Movement (SLM) and Sudan Liberation Army (SLA). The government creates a plan to use the Janjaweed to fight rebels. The Janjaweed begins to focus attacks on civilians.

2004 Widespread reporting of Darfur genocide. Organizations and individuals begin to urge government action to halt the genocide.

2005 The SLA breaks apart into separate units.

2006 The government and one SLA unit sign Darfur Peace Agreement (DPA). DPA fails to end the fighting.

2007 New peace talks begin between Khartoum and rebel leaders. Main rebel leaders refuse to attend. Rebels attack African Union (AU) peacekeepers, killing several. Soldiers and the Janjaweed respond with attacks on towns.

GLOSSARY

Arabization The process of turning a country into a place for Arabs only.

atrocity A wicked, brutal, or cruel act.

barbarity Extreme cruelty.

coalition An alliance of groups for joint action.

coup The violent overthrow of a government by a small group.

desertification The process of land that was not originally desert turning into desert.

dictator One who exercises supreme authority in a country, usually without having been elected to do so.

ethnic Having to do with large groups of people classed according to common racial, national, tribal, religious, linguistic, or cultural origin or background.

extremist A person who promotes extreme political or religious ideas and does not tolerate other views.

guerrilla Describing a small, defensive force of irregular soldiers.

Islamist A person who promotes Islamization.

Islamization The process of making something Islamic.

jihad A holy war fought as a religious duty to spread Islam.

manifesto A document that makes public the beliefs and intentions of a group of people.

mosque A place of worship and prayer for Muslims.

Nazi A member of or having to do with the German political party led by Adolf Hitler during World War II.

nomad A person who moves from place to place.

Nuremberg Trials Trials held in Nuremberg, Germany, from 1945 to 1949 to judge leaders of Germany for their actions during World War II.

op-ed A column on a page of special features opposite the editorial page of a newspaper. Short for "opposite editorial."

propaganda Ideas spread whether they are true or not to support a cause or to hurt an opposing cause.

rape The act of using force to make a person have sex.

sheikh An Arab chief or tribal leader.

supremacist A person who promotes the false idea that one group of people is superior to others.

visa Document providing permission from government authorities to enter a country.

FOR MORE INFORMATION

Darfur Relief and Documentation Centre (DRDC)
Crêts-de-Pregny 27
1218 Grand-Saconnex
Geneva, Switzerland
Web site: http://www.darfurcentre.ch

> The DRDC is a nongovernmental organization (NGO) founded in
> 2004 to work with people from Darfur and other parts of the world
> to find a way to help Darfur's people end the violence and rebuild
> their lives. It also maintains a database of groups, researchers, and
> academics from Darfur.

Doctors Without Borders
U.S. Headquarters
333 7th Avenue, 2nd Floor
New York, NY 10001-5004
(212) 679-6800
Web site: http://www.doctorswithoutborders.org

> Doctors Without Borders is an NGO that provides medical aid around
> the world in response to conflict and natural disasters. It is active in
> Darfur, and its Web site provides information about the genocide there.

Genocide Intervention Network
1333 H Street NW, First Floor
Washington, DC 20005
(202) 481-8220
Web site: http://www.genocideintervention.net

> The Genocide Intervention Network is devoted to educating people
> about genocide and what they can do to stop it. It also provides
> information on fund-raising and events around the country.

International Rescue Committee
122 East 42nd Street
New York, NY 10168-1289
(212) 551-3000
Web site: http://www.theirc.org
  Founded in 1933, the International Rescue Committee is an NGO
  that serves refugees and communities victimized by oppression or
  violent conflict worldwide. It is active in Darfur, and its Web site
  provides information about the genocide there.

Oxfam Canada
250 City Centre Avenue, Suite 400
Ottawa, ON K1R 6K7
Canada
(613) 237-5236
Web site: http://www.oxfam.ca
  Oxfam Canada is an NGO that works to end poverty and injustice in
  countries around the world. It is active in Darfur, and its Web site
  includes information about the genocide there.

Res Publica
Darfur Advocacy Project
260 Fifth Avenue, 9th Floor
New York, NY 10001
Web site: http://www.darfurgenocide.org
  The Darfur Advocacy Project provides news and information about
  Darfur, as well as suggestions for actions people can take to help end
  the genocide in Darfur.

Save Darfur Canada
P.O. Box 56094
Montreal, QC H3Z 3G3

Canada
(514) 935-8806
Web site: http://www.savedarfurcanada.org
   Save Darfur Canada acts as an information and networking resource
   for individuals and groups across Canada.

Save Darfur Coalition
2120 L Street NW, Suite 335
Washington, DC 20037
(800) 917-2034
Web site: http://www.savedarfur.org
   The Save Darfur Coalition's mission is to raise public awareness
   about the situation in Darfur and get people to take action to halt
   the genocide.

United States Holocaust Memorial Museum
100 Raoul Wallenberg Place SW
Washington, DC 20024-2126
(202) 488-0400
Web site: http://www.ushmm.org
   The United States Holocaust Memorial Museum is a living memorial
   to the Holocaust of World War II. Its Web site provides information
   about genocide in general and about the genocide in Darfur in
   particular.

WEB SITES

Due to the changing nature of Internet links, Rosen Publishing has
developed an online list of Web sites related to the subject of this book.
This site is updated regularly. Please use this link to access the list:

http://www.rosenlinks.com/gmt/geda

FOR FURTHER READING

Cooper, John. *Raphael Lemkin and the Struggle for the Genocide Convention*. New York, NY: Palgrave Macmillan, 2008.

Des Chenes, Elizabeth, ed. *Genocide*. Farmington Hills, MI: Greenhaven Press, 2007.

Gifford, Clive, et al. *Refugees*. London, England: Belitha Press Ltd., 2002.

Hecht, Joan. *The Journey of the Lost Boys*. Jacksonville, FL: Allswell Press, 2005.

January, Brendan. *Genocide: Modern Crimes Against Humanity*. Minneapolis, MN: Twenty-First Century Books, 2006.

Kavanaugh, Dorothy. *Sudan*. Broomall, PA: Mason Crest Publishers, 2007.

Nnoromele, Salome C. *Sudan*. San Diego, CA: Lucent Books, 2004.

Springer, Jane. *Genocide*. Toronto, ON, Canada: Groundwood Books, 2006.

Xavier, John. *Darfur: African Genocide*. New York, NY: Rosen Publishing Group, 2007.

BIBLIOGRAPHY

Assyrian International News Agency. "Amid Escalating Fear of Massacres, Assyrians Commemorate Martyr's Day." Retrieved September 23, 2007 (http://www.aina.org/releases/20040807203428.htm).

The Avalon Project at Yale Law School. "Nuremberg Trial Proceedings, Vol. 1, Indictment: Count Three." Retrieved October 4, 2007 (http://www.yale.edu/lawweb/avalon/imt/proc/count3.htm).

BBC News. "Rwanda: How the Genocide Happened." Retrieved September 22, 2007 (http://news.bbc.co.uk/2/hi/africa/1288230.stm).

Berenbaum, Michael. "Holocaust." *World Book Multimedia Encyclopedia*. Chicago, IL: World Book, Inc., 2001.

Britannica Online Encyclopedia. "Crusades: The Albigensian Crusade." Retrieved September 19, 2007 (http://www.britannica.com/eb/article-235535/Crusades).

Britannica Online Encyclopedia. "Genocide." Retrieved September 19, 2007 (http://www.britannica.com/eb/article-9036419/genocide#283846.hook).

Britannica Online Encyclopedia. "International Criminal Court." Retrieved September 19, 2007 (http://www.britannica.com/eb/article-9390314/International-Criminal-Court#786622.hook).

Cheadle, Don, and John Prendergast. *Not on Our Watch*. New York, NY: Hyperion, 2007.

Commission for Historical Clarification. "Guatemala: Memory of Silence." *Report of the Commission for Historical Clarification: Conclusions and Recommendations*. Retrieved September 22, 2007 (http://shr.aaas.org/guatemala/ceh/report/english/toc.html).

Daly, M. W. *Darfur's Sorrow: A History of Destruction and Genocide*. New York, NY: Cambridge University Press, 2007.

EuropaWorld. "Raphael Lemkin." Retrieved September 19, 2007 (http://www.europaworld.org/issue40/raphaellemkin22601.htm).

Flint, Julie, and Alex de Waal. *Darfur: A Short History of a Long War.*
London, England: Zed Books Ltd., 2005.
Gavin, Philip. "Genocide in the 20th Century: Armenians in Turkey,
1915–1918." The History Place. Retrieved September 23, 2007 (http://
www.historyplace.com/worldhistory/genocide/armenians.htm).
HistoryWorld. "History of the Peloponnesian Wars." Retrieved
September 22, 2007 (http://www.historyworld.net/wrldhis/
PlainTextHistories.asp?historyid=ac46).
International Crisis Group. "Conflict History: Sudan." Retrieved
September 20, 2007 (http://www.crisisgroup.org/home/index.cfm?
action=conflict_search&l=1&t=1&c_country=101).
The International Tribunal for the Former Yugoslavia. "Case No. IT-95-
5-I: The Prosecutor of the Tribunal Against Radovan Karadzic, Ratko
Mladic." Retrieved September 22, 2007 (http://www.un.org/icty/
indictment/english/kar-ii950724e.htm).
Lemarchand, Rene. "Chad." *World Book Multimedia Encyclopedia.*
Chicago, IL: World Book, Inc., 2002.
Office of the High Commissioner for Human Rights. "Convention on
the Prevention and Punishment of the Crime of Genocide."
Retrieved September 19, 2007 (http://www.unhchr.ch/html/menu3/
b/p_genoci.htm).
Perkins, Kenneth J. "Sudan." *World Book Multimedia Encyclopedia.*
Chicago, IL: World Book, Inc., 2001.
Pham, J. Peter. "REM: Islamist Terrorist Regime in Khartoum." *World
Defense Review*, June 1, 2006. Retrieved October 26, 2007 (http://
www.defenddemocracy.org/in_the_media/in_the_media_show.htm?
doc_id=375101).
Pranger, Robert J. "Genocide." *World Book Multimedia Encyclopedia.*
Chicago, IL: World Book, Inc., 2001.
Prevent Genocide International. "Ongoing Actions." Retrieved
September 19, 2007 (http://www.preventgenocide.org).

Rummel, R. J. "Genocide." University of Hawaii System. Retrieved September 19, 2007 (http://www.hawaii.edu/powerkills/GENOCIDE.ENCY.HTM).

Steidle, Brian, and Gretchen Steidle Wallace. *The Devil Came on Horseback*. New York, NY: PublicAffairs, 2007.

United Human Rights Council. "Cambodia Genocide (Pol Pot)." Retrieved October 4, 2007 (http://www.unitedhumanrights.org/Genocide/pol_pot.htm).

Ward, Dan Sewell. "The Albigensian Crusade." Library of Halexandria. Retrieved September 19, 2007 (http://www.halexandria.org/dward220.htm).

INDEX

ABOUT THE AUTHOR

Janey Levy is an editor and author who lives in Colden, New York. She has written more than seventy-five books for young people. She regularly supports the work of the International Rescue Committee and Doctors Without Borders, two of the major organizations helping Darfur's refugees and IDPs.

PHOTO CREDITS

Cover (top), pp. 4 (left), 7, 14, 24, 32, 41 Jose Cendon/AFP/Getty Images; cover (bottom), p. 33 Scott Nelson/Getty Images; pp. 4–5 Cris Bouroncle/AFP/Getty Images; p. 8 © Bettmann/Corbis; p. 9 The Art Archive/Bibliothèque Nationale Paris; pp. 11, 13, 30, 38, 39, 42, 47 © AP Images; p. 15 © Geoatlas; p. 17 Scott Peterson/Liaison/Getty Images; pp. 19, 37 © Liba Taylor/Corbis; p. 20 Str/AFP/Getty Images; p. 22 Joel Robine/AFP/Getty Images; p. 26 Espen Rasmussen/AFP/Getty Images; p. 27 Scott Nelson/Getty Images; pp. 28, 34 Desirey Minkoh/AFP/Getty Images; p. 43 Nicholas Roberts/AFP/Getty Images; p. 46 Melanie Stetson Freeman/The Christian Science Monitor/Getty Images; p. 48 Isam Al-Haj/AFP/Getty Images.

Designer: Tahara Anderson; Photo Researcher: Cindy Reiman